31 Days of Focus

RENITA COLLINS

St. Clair Shores, Michigan

31 Days of Focus

Unless otherwise indicated, Bible quotations are taken from the KJV version of the Bible. Copyright © 1994 by Zondervan

Take note that the name satan and associated names are not capitalized.

We choose not to acknowledge him, even to the point of violating grammatical rules.

ISBN (13) 978-0-9799646-0-2
ISBN (10) 0-9799646-0-1

Printed in the United States of America.

*31 Days Of Focus is dedicated to my dad,
Ramon Ellis, who was always focused on
his God-given goals and dreams.*

Acknowledgements

To the love of my life, my wonderful husband, *Frank Collins Jr.*, thanks for working so hard to keep stability, love and laughter in our home. You are the best and I am honored to be your wife! Also to my son, *Frank Collins III*, my promise from God, you always brighten my day and remind me that one of my reasons for living is to be your mommy! Finally, to my beautiful mother, *Barbara Ellis*, thank you for always believing in me and being my number one fan!

Table of Contents

Introduction

Life is filled with seasons of change and growth. This book was written during a time of transition in my life. I realized that God was trying to lead me in a different direction. God had instructed me to leave the place where I was working and begin working from home. He had also instructed me to enter a time of intense prayer and fasting.

Little did I know that God was preparing me for a series of events. Shortly after leaving my place of employment, my husband let me know that he had been in prayer and God had revealed to him that it was time for us to start a new church. Soon after starting the church, I became pregnant after years of trying to conceive. I wrote several songs of praise and worship. God instructed me to start a ministry for women and girls. He also told me that I would write a book. This was definitely a season of major change and growth!

During this season, after daily prayer, I would listen carefully for further instructions from the Lord. Every time I would hear from Him I would write down His words of wisdom, as well as my own thoughts, so that I could refer back to them anytime.

This book is a result of 31 days of intense focus and prayer. The words of wisdom and direction that I received during this time were such a blessing and inspiration to me that I decided to share them with you, praying that you will be blessed and inspired as well!

It is my sincere hope that you will step out in faith and accomplish that which you are compelled to do. With God all things are possible! You know what you must do; but it requires **faith and action**. I pray that you will take this 31-day journey and allow your faith to stretch you beyond **your** limits.

Your partner in the journey,

Renita

Day 1

"WHAT ARE YOU WAITING FOR, DO IT NOW!

Ready, Set, Go…

So many times in life we have false starts just like in a track meet. We start running then we realize we have to go back because we "jumped the gun." Other times we can never get out of the "ready" or "set" position.

You know what it is that you must do, it has already been revealed to you, even if it's just a glimpse. You must now simply ask God for wisdom, make a decision, and DO IT! You may say "It's not that simple!" It may not be "easy," but it is simple. Any time you have to do something that is different from what you have been doing, it is not always easy; but all it takes is a "simple" decision. What comes natural is to do what is comfortable, what feels good, or what is easy; however, you were not necessarily called to do what is easy but to do what is right. So get up, do it now, don't hesitate. Pray for wisdom (ready), make a decision (set), and DO IT (GO)!

Father, today I ask that you will give me wisdom and knowledge in the following areas: _____

_____

_____

Challenge: I challenge you today to resist the desire to fulfill the lusts of the flesh, be it overeating, sexual immorality, or just plain laziness. Also, resist the tendency to fulfill the desires of the unsurrendered mind, be it fear, or even complacency. Seek the face of God, ask for wisdom and obey His direction.

Prayer: *Father I thank you that I no longer walk according to the course of this world, fulfilling the desires of my flesh and my mind. I now, by your grace and great love for me, walk according to the course that you prepared for me (Ephesians 2:1-7).*

Confession: *I will walk in the spirit and I will not fulfill the lust of my flesh (Galatians 5:16).*(repeat at least 3 times today)

Notes

Notes

Day 2

WHAT ARE THE OBSTACLES IN YOUR WAY?

One morning while I was out for a walk, I was not paying attention to the ground or what was around me. Suddenly, I found myself tripping over a large crack in the sidewalk. I later encountered a barricade that blocked the sidewalk because the cement was being repaired. Also, there were puddles from the earlier rain, over which I had to leap to prevent splashing myself.

As we walk through this life's journey, we will encounter "cracks," "barricades," and "puddles." The idea is not to stop, but keep moving! You must either go around, or step over them. However, in order to recognize them, you must be **alert** to the warnings of the Holy Spirit.

Sometimes our greatest obstacles to overcome is **OURSELVES**. We must allow our mind, will and emotions (our soul) to line up with the mind and will of God.

Do not allow yourself to become acquainted with complacency or fear. These two mindsets will paralyze you and keep you from moving forward in any area of your life. Acquaint yourself with perseverance, long-suffering and faith.

Identify your obstacles, find out if there is a lesson to learn, then keep moving. Be alert to the Holy Spirit's promptings. Make a decision to go forward with perseverance to the end.

THE LORD HAS NEED OF RUNNERS IN THIS RACE OF LIFE THAT WILL ENDURE TO THE END!

Identify Obstacles (including yourself) _____

_____

_____

_____

How will you go around or leap over them?

_____

_____

Is there a lesson to learn?_____

_____

Prayer: *Father, in the name of Jesus I ask that you would renew a steadfast spirit within me. Lord I place my trust in You. Uphold my steps in your paths that my footsteps may not slip (Psalm 51:10, Psalm 17:5)*

Scriptures to Meditate: Psalm 51:10, Psalm 17:5

Notes

Notes

Notes

Day 3

STAY FOCUSED

The stake out!

In a stake out, the undercover detectives must watch in order to observe the habits or the movements of the suspect. They must stay alert so that they do not miss an opportunity to apprehend the suspect. This requires great focus and discipline. The detectives must resist the urge to sleep when they should be watching!

Have you ever been in a perpetual state of "spiritual sleep," when you should be "watching?" You must resist the urge to sleep and remain alert. The Word of God admonishes us to "Watch and Pray." Sleeping will cause you to miss opportunity.

WAKE UP AND GET FOCUSED!

The following habits will cause you to remain alert and focused: **fasting, prayer, meditation on God's Word, simplifying your life, eliminating unnecessary activities, seeking His face, then listening to His voice.**

One who is focused..............
1. Knows his/her assignment
2. Has a plan of action
3. Has begun preparation for implementing the plan

FOCUS REQUIRES DESIRE, DISCIPLINE, AND DETERMINATION. You must first have a desire to fulfill your goal. Once desire has taken root, discipline and determination are two states of the mind that will cause you to be compelled to accomplish the task.

What is your assignment?_____

_____

_____

_____

What is your plan of action?_____

_____

When will you begin implementing the plan?_____

_____

Prayer: *Father, in the name of Jesus I ask that you would help me to walk circumspectly, remaining alert and focused in order to fulfill the call. (Ephesians 5:15)*

Confession: *The Lord is my strength and I can do all things through Him. (Psalm 27:1, Philippians 4:13)*

Notes

Notes

Notes

Day 4

AVOID THE DISTRACTION OF BUSYNESS

Are you busy or productive?

We must all guard ourselves against the "trap" of busyness. Having too many commitments in your schedule will cause you to choke the life out of those things that are most important.

This is the "Hierarchy of Priority"
1. Relationship with God (not church activities)
2. Husband/Wife
3. Children
4. Job/Vocation/Extended Family

Answer the following questions:

1. How much time are you spending at the top of the chart?

2. Is your daily devotion time rushed, or do you some times skip it altogether?

3. Are you aware of the needs and concerns of your spouse and children and are you actively serving them?

4. Are you so tired at the end of the day that you have neither the energy nor the patience to help your children with their homework?

5. Is your mind so consumed that you find it difficult to sit and listen to your children as they discuss their day with you?

6. Is the distance between you and your spouse becoming greater because your only interaction is a rushed greeting in the morning, and a tired kiss goodnight? Maybe you just sit dazed in front of the television when you could pick up a book or call a friend to give an encouraging word.

Did any of these questions cause you to become convicted; if so, just repent, do not fall into condemnation. Today is your opportunity to start in a new direction!

Answer the following questions:

In what areas of my life do I need to spend more quality time developing? _____

_____

_____

What are the extra curricular activities in which I am involved?

_____

_____

_____

Which of these (activities) are propelling me closer
to my destiny/goal or cultivating my most important
relationships(God, Spouse, Children, Family)?

_____

_____

_____

Confession: *God is my source, and my strength. My
relationship with God is my top priority. I will see to it that
every area of my life reflects this statement.*

Notes

Notes

Notes

Day 5

CONFIDENCE IN CHRIST

"But the Lord is faithful, who will establish you and guard you…." (2 Thessalonians 3:3)

In all that we do, we must place our hope and confidence in Christ. His word says that we are not to cast away our confidence (Hebrews 10:35). We must remain committed and realize everything we are and ever hope to be is in Him! After we have remained committed to fulfilling the will of God, we will receive what God has promised (Hebrews 10:36).

So remember do not throw away your confidence, stay committed to your purpose **no matter what!** God rewards those who remain confident in Him.

Confession: *I place my confidence in the Most High God. I will stand on His Word, knowing that He will accomplish for me what he has promised.*

Scriptures to Meditate: Hebrews 10:35-36, Hebrews 11:1, 2 Thessalonians 3:3

Notes

Notes

Day 6

STAND ON HIS PROMISES

God's Word will not go out from Him and return to Him void, but it will fulfill His purposes (Isaiah 55:11). If God said it, you can stand on it! His Word is a foundation that has no cracks in it! It is solid, it is true, it will stand any test and it will not change.

What is God saying to you regarding your individual situation? If you have not already done so, take the time to seek God concerning your decisions. Seek Him concerning that mate or child you desire. Seek Him regarding that promotion or business opportunity. Whatever it is that you desire of Him, ask, then take the time to listen. When God has given you His Word concerning your situation, be sure that you allow Him to work on your behalf. You may still be a work in progress.

You must be properly prepared for your season. Seeds must be planted, properly rooted and watered before they begin to grow. This process may be either short or long, depending on the "ground" in which the seeds are planted. Some ground may contain old roots that must be uprooted before new ones can be cultivated. Some ground must be fertilized in order to produce fruit. Others must be tilled in order to break up the soil to produce growth. The ground in this analogy represents your heart! You must allow God to prepare the "ground of your heart" no matter how long the process may take.

Don't do anything to hinder His plan! Allow Him to show Himself strong on your behalf. You can rest assured that what He has promised He will bring to pass. It may not happen in the sequence of events that you conceive in your **human** mind, but it will come to pass. Remember, He is able to do exceedingly, abundantly, above all we could even ask or think (Ephesians 3:20). So, having done all to stand, continue to stand on His Word (Ephesians 6:13-14).

Pray Aloud: *Father, today I seek Your face. Your Word says that You are a rewarder of those who diligently seek You.*

Let Your perfect will be accomplished in my life. I surrender Lord. Please take full control of my life. I place all of my trust and confidence in You. Amen

Scriptures to Meditate: Ephesians 6:10-18

Answer the following question:

What decisions are you facing right now?

Notes

Notes

Day 7

DWELLING IN HIS PRESENCE

There is absolute security and peace in the presence of God. There is no other place you can go to experience this level of peace and security. God desires to fellowship with you, that is why He created you.

Make an effort today to spend some extra time alone with God. Spend an extra five minutes in the shower or tub. Put the kids to bed early, turn off the television, turn off the ringer on your home and cellular phone or pager. Arrive at work a few minutes before everyone else arrives. Take the long way home and turn off the radio in the car. There are several ways to carve out extra time with God, but **you** must make the effort.

Quality time with God fills your "tank" and allows you to pour into others. To ensure that your tank is not close to empty, take this opportunity to allow God to fill you today!

Scripture to Meditate: Psalm 8, Psalm 103:1-5, Psalm 139

List ways to carve out extra time with God today.

Notes

Day 8

DO NOT WORRY!

"Therefore I say to you do not worry......" (Matthew 6:25)

Guilt and worry are two states of mind that will rob you of an awareness of God's presence as well as His sovereignty. Guilt and worry cause you to be self-centered instead of God-focused. Do not become obsessed with the overwhelming feelings of these two states of mind. Take authority and command that these strongholds over your mind are destroyed (2 Corinthians 10:4-5). Allow your thoughts to remain focused upon the Prince of Peace.

Worrying cannot change any situation, but it can negatively change your faith!

Prayer: *Father, in the name of Jesus, I take authority over my mind and I command that every stronghold, argument, or any obstacle that would prevent me from knowing the truth about You or Your Word, would be destroyed. I will allow my mind to cling to those thoughts that are in line with Your Word. Amen*

Scriptures to Meditate: Matthew 6:25-34, Philippians 4:6-7

Notes

Day 9

I SURRENDER!

Do you know what it means to surrender? You must **voluntarily** relinquish control. It is not about what is easy, and convenient, or what pleases your flesh; but it is about what God wants.

Surrender includes giving up the possession of something into the power of another according to Webster's Dictionary. Surrendering is not allowing your flesh to control you, but allowing the Holy Spirit to control every aspect of your being including your body and soul (mind, will, and emotions). For instance, your body may want to sleep when you need to get up and pray. Your mind may be filled with thoughts that contradict the Word of God. Your emotions may cause you to lash out at someone when you are commanded to walk in love. Your will may suggest that you overindulge in unhealthy foods and avoid exercise. All of these instances are examples of a body or soul that is not surrendered.

You must allow the power of the Holy Spirit to take control of your life! Let His agenda become your agenda. The "what, when, why and how" must be surrendered to Him. God will immensely bless you and give you the desires of your heart when you conform to His plan and His timing. Do not give thought to the how, why and when, just leave that to Him. Concentrate on the "what" that God has instructed you to do and do it no matter how you feel or think! Let your focus be obedience and surrender.

Scriptures to Meditate: Romans 12:1, Philippians 4:8, Romans 8:5

Confession: *I WILL WALK IN THE SPIRIT AND NOT FULFILL THE LUST OF MY FLESH! (Galatians 5:16)*

Notes

Notes

Day 10

GET UP AND GET BACK ON TRACK!

If you ever get to a point in your journey where you "fall off" the track or you make a "wrong turn," then immediately get up and get back on track! This situation may occur throughout your journey; however, do not meditate on the fact that you have lost focus, the important thing is to get back on track.

"For a righteous man may fall seven times and rise again…" (Proverbs 24:16). Do not allow yourself to be plagued by condemnation. If you find yourself sidetracked in any area of your life, repent and get back on the right road. God is a loving and forgiving God who will continue to love and forgive those who fear Him.

Do not allow imaginations and high things to exalt themselves against the truth about God (2 Corinthians 10:5). Cast those thoughts down, get up and shake off condemnation. Regain your focus and trust in God; then continue forward!

Prayer: *Father, I ask that you would forgive me for not continuing on the path that you set before me. Father, I thank you that there is no condemnation to those who are in Christ Jesus, who walk according to the spirit and not the flesh. Father, I will walk in the spirit, continuing in Your path. I thank You Father for Your grace. Amen*

Scriptures to Meditate: Psalm 16:9-11, Romans 8:1-2

Notes

Day 11

FAITH

What is your level of commitment even when your mind or your body is feeling "contrary?" Are you able to trust God even when in your mind you want to be depressed? Are you able to believe that good things are going to happen when you are in the middle of a crisis? "All things are possible to him who believes" (Mark 9:23). This is what **Jesus** said!

In any automobile, a series of tests must be conducted in order to prove that the product can stand the test of time, adverse weather, and even crashes. You are just like that automobile! Faith is enduring the test knowing that you will come off the "assembly line" perfect and mature. Faith is knowing that ultimately God is in control of your life as you cast your cares on Him.

For the Lord said, "*as you pass through the waters, I will be with you; and through the rivers, they shall not overflow you. When you walk through the fire, you shall not be burned, nor shall the flame scorch you. For I am the Lord your God...*" (Isaiah 43:2-4).

Confession: *I have the faith to say to any mountain "be removed and be cast into the sea..." (Mark 11:23)*
I have the faith to believe that all things are possible (Mark 9:23)
I have faith that the unseen promises of God shall come to pass (Hebrews 11:1)
I have faith that pleases God (Hebrews 11:6)
My unwavering trust and my hope are in the unchanging, all knowing, omnipresent, all powerful, God of my salvation.

I WILL NOT BE MOVED! TODAY AND EVERYDAY I WILL STAND STRONG!

Notes

Notes

Day 12

THERE IS MORE TO YOU

THAN MEETS THE EYE!

Every one of us is born with a certain set of tools to assist us in fulfilling our destiny. Some are more outgoing, while others are more reserved. Some love excitement, while others are more cautious. Some are natural leaders, while others are effective team players.

The challenge is that since we are born with a blank slate and often unaware of how to use the "operating instructions" available to us, (God's Word and the Holy Spirit) we are left to our own devices to figure out the proper path. Another challenge is that because our slate is blank, we often become "written on" by external conditions including our environment, life experiences and family. These external conditions usually contradict who God says we are. We often allow the criticism and abuse of others to shape our opinion of who we are. What we must do is create another clean slate and only allow **God** to write who we are and what we are capable of accomplishing through Him. We must then take our instruction book, the Word of God, and follow its directives!

From this day forward, if you have not already done so, present yourself to God and allow Him to "clean" your slate and fill you with a renewed sense of who you are and your capabilities in Him. Submit yourself to Him. I mean truly submit **WHOLEHEARTEDLY!**

Scriptures to Meditate: 2 Corinthians 5:17, Isaiah 43:18-19

Notes

Notes

Day 13

I AM WHO GOD SAYS I AM!

What does God's Word say about you? What does His Word say about your particular circumstances? God's Word gives several promises to the believer who fears Him and keeps His commandments. Deuteronomy 30:15 states, *"See, I have set before you today life and good, death and evil, in that I command you today to love the Lord your God, to walk in His ways, and to keep His commandments, His statutes, and His judgements, that you may live and multiply; and the Lord your God will bless you in the land which you go to possess."* Deuteronomy 28 gives a list of blessings that shall "overtake" you if you obey the voice of the Lord.

Did you know that you are a "special treasure" to God (Deuteronomy 7:6)? He loves you and has chosen you to be a part of His kingdom, loving and serving Him all the days of your life! "You are the salt of the earth" (Matt 5:13). God has called you to add flavor to your surroundings and not be "trampled under the foot of men." Do your surroundings reflect your flavor or have you lost your "saltiness." God has called you to influence those around you for His glory. How else will they "taste and see that the Lord is good" (Psalm 34:8).

Come out of your prayer closet and allow the power of God to be manifested through you so that the world would come to Him!

Scriptures to Meditate: Deuteronomy 7:6-11, Matthew 5:13-16, 1 Peter 2:9

Answer the following question:

Who does God say that I am? -

Notes

Day 14

YOU ARE MY HIDING PLACE

In Psalm 32, David addresses the Lord saying, "You are my hiding place, you shall preserve me from trouble…" Have you ever felt like David did in this passage? If there is a time when you are afraid or uncertain, you can run to the Lord and He will receive you and give you instruction. In verse 8 of this passage, God responds to those who run to Him saying, "I will teach you in the way you should go."

Learn to respond immediately to the direction of the Lord. We are not to be like the stubborn horse or the mule who must wear a harness in order to be directed by its rider. We must respond immediately on our own to God's instruction.

Are you a stubborn mule who has to be forced to do what is right, or are you one who runs to God, seeks direction, and responds quickly to His instruction? Examine yourself this day and allow your mind to be renewed by the Word of God.

Scriptures to Meditate: Psalm 32:7-11, Psalm 61:1-4, Proverbs 3:5-6, Proverbs 18:10

Notes

63

Notes

Day 15

SPEAK THOSE THINGS

"Death and life are in the power of the tongue..." Proverbs 18:21. If there is anything in your life that is dead or dying, you have the power in the name of Jesus to speak life! Take a moment to examine your life, your current circumstances, your current state of mind, your level of faith. Are you living according to the Word of the Lord? Are you living based on who God says you are and the power that you possess in the Name of Jesus!

What are the mountains in your life? Are they your own thoughts or fears? By faith, speak to them and command them to be cast into the sea. God is bigger than your mindset, He has the power to change your circumstances. He has given you authority to take up serpents. The power that lies within you is activated when you speak in faith.

Today begin to speak those things that be not as though they were. Allow the power of God to miraculously change your circumstances. No longer shall you speak death. No longer will you say what you cannot do. No longer will you focus on what you do not have. No more focusing on the symptoms. Speak those things! Declare victory in Jesus Name!

Challenge: For the rest of the day, maintain an attitude of praise and thanksgiving toward God. Thank Him for your victory!

Confession: *I DECLARE IT, I DECREE IT, I COMMAND IT, I CAN SEE IT, VICTORY!*

Scripture to Meditate: Proverbs 18:21

Notes

Notes

Day 16

ENJOYING HIS PRESENCE

"In Your presence is fullness of joy" (Psalm 16:11). "Where the spirit of the Lord is, there is liberty" (2 Corinthians 3:17). In the presence of the Lord there is freedom from condemnation. God accepts you just as you are with all your imperfections and He says, **Come to ME**, so that you might be cleansed and made perfect. When you enter the Holy Place, you experience an incomparable fullness of joy! Once you have been in the presence of the Lord, you are changed forever. Just as Moses had a glow when the Israelites saw him after he had been in God's presence, you too will have a glow from being in His presence.

Notes

Day 17

ACKNOWLEDGE HIM

"In all thy ways acknowledge Him…" Proverbs 3:6. The opposite of acknowledge is ignore. See to it that you are not ignoring God but acknowledging Him. Acknowledge His presence throughout the day. If your best friend decided to spend the day with you, would you just ignore him/her the entire time, never having any conversation or interaction? Absolutely not! So how can you ignore the presence of the Most High God, Emanuel, God with us, Jehovah Shamah!

Make it a point to acknowledge Him throughout your day. He is your true friend. Talk to Him and allow

Him to talk to you. Express your joys and your concerns with Him. He cares for you! Include Him in all of your decision-making. Ask Him for daily wisdom.

After the resurrection and ascension of Jesus, He sent the comforter, who is God the Holy Spirit, to lead us into all truth. The Holy Spirit is God and He is ready and willing to commune with you but you must acknowledge Him!

Scriptures to Meditate: Proverbs 3:6

Notes

Notes

Day 18

APPRECIATION

Today I wanted to do something to show my husband how much I appreciate him; no particular occasion or reason, just because. While I was in the dollar store, I saw a certificate that read, "Number One, Cream of the Crop…." There were lots of words that edified the recipient. I said, "That's it; that's him!" I think my husband is the best husband, father and friend, the list goes on! I wanted him to know beyond any doubt that I am his number one fan! When he opened the envelope, his smile brightened the whole room. His smile made me smile too. I said to myself, "That is how I want to honor my Lord."

The Lord delights in the praises of His people. We should go out of our way to let Him know how much we love and appreciate Him. We must offer Him our sacrifice of praise. I can relate to David when he says, "I will bless the Lord at all times" (Psalm 34:1). Our desire should be to make our heavenly Father smile.

Challenge: How many ways today can you show God how much you appreciate Him. Go out of your way to share His goodness with a neighbor or coworker. Find someone in need and bless them. He alone is truly worthy of honor every day of our lives!

Scriptures to Meditate: Psalm 8:1, Psalm 9:1-2, Psalm 34:1-3

List the names of individuals who you will bless today.

Notes

Day 19

IT'S NOT ABOUT YOU!

Be unselfish!

How many times have you done something that you did not want to do in order to help someone else? Today I had planned to go to an intercessory prayer meeting and service that was going to last half of the day. The next day, we were going to be hosting a Father's Day Dinner at our church and we had asked my in-laws to barbeque chicken and ribs for us. I should let you know that my in-laws are 89 and 90 years old. No one was available to help them and my husband was working; so that left me. My initial thought was, "But it's my day off. I wanted to sleep in, and I hate cleaning and cutting meat."

Then I started to spiritualize the situation thinking I needed to go to intercessory prayer because I would be much more effective in prayer for our people rather than cleaning and cooking meat.

Then finally, after my soul finished with the ultimate pity party, the Holy Spirit spoke to me and said, *"Stop being so selfish!"* Wow, that hit me like a ton of bricks! I immediately repented. I would be much more effective relieving them of their burden in the natural than just praying for them! I never want to have a self-righteous, self-centered attitude. It certainly does not glorify God.

So many times we are fooled into thinking that being involved in several church or community activities is much more effective than simply coming home and cooking dinner for our spouse, spending an afternoon playing with our children or going to help a friend move into a new home. It is so easy to get caught up in "self advancement." One day you will look around and you will have that degree, promotion, community service award, or successful business. You will not realize that you missed your daughter's first dance recital, or you may ignore the signs of your son experimenting with drugs. Your spouse may seem like a stranger. Now what! Was it all worth it?

God commands us to love our neighbor as ourselves. Who is your neighbor? Your closest neighbor on earth is your family and you are to love them by serving them. This is total unselfishness.

Scriptures to Meditate: James 2:14-26

Notes

Notes

Day 20

DE-CLUTTER YOUR ENVIRONMENT

Have you ever been in a cluttered environment and felt uneasy or overwhelmed? Sometimes you can walk into a room filled with clutter and you don't know where to begin cleaning. In the midst of clutter, you often feel unproductive. This concept is also true in your daily life. If you participate in too may activities, you can become overwhelmed and ultimately unproductive. You must ask yourself the question, "Am I productive or just busy?"

Make it a point this week to de-clutter your environment…

Get rid of those thoughts that exalt themselves against the knowledge of God.

• Release those friendships that drain the life out of you and hold on to those that sharpen you!

• Cancel all activities that simply consume your time and energy and only participate in those that propel you toward your destiny.

• Give away any clothes in your closet that you have not worn in 365 days.

• Create a filing system to organize all of your important papers.

• Keep all rooms in your house decorated with **simple** elegance.

• Keep your car clean and in order, inside and out.

ALLOW YOUR IMMEDIATE SURROUNDINGS TO REFLECT THE GLORY OF GOD!
When you de-clutter your life inside and out, you will find a level of peace and productivity you never imagined!

I challenge you today to examine **all** areas of your life and begin to release anything that is hindering you in any way. De-clutter your surroundings and focus on those things that are of absolute top priority.

Scriptures to Meditate: Proverbs 21:5, 2 Corinthians 10:5, Ephesians 1:5, Philippians 4:8

List any unnecessary activities that are consuming your time. In what ways can you de-clutter your surroundings?

Notes

Day 21

GETTING PROPER REST

When a cellular or cordless phone has been off its charger for too long, it sends a signal indicating that a recharge is required. Sometimes it is even difficult to hear the person on the other end; you may even lose the call all together. Our bodies need recharging on a regular basis just like our cellular and cordless phones. That recharge that we so desperately need is called REST! Your body will send you a signal that your "charge" is running low. If you ignore the signal, you will lose your "charge" completely, and you do not want that to happen! Please do not ignore the signals.

Many of us fill our lives with so much activity and

never stop to consider our need for the proper amount of rest. Most of the activity in which we are participating is either unnecessary or untimely. Stop now and ask God two questions

> - *Are the activities in which I participate of top priority?*
> - *Is this something that I should be doing at this time in my life?*

Sit down and assess your activities according to this hierarchy of priorities.

1. Relationship with God
2. Spouse
3. Children
4. Job/Vocation/Ministry/Extended Family/Friends

Tell yourself that it is okay to rest. It is okay to take an hour, a day, or even an entire week to do absolutely nothing but rest!

If your body has been signaling you to recharge, take time now and adjust your schedule so that you can get the proper rest. When you take time to rest, you will be much more **effective** in your journey of life.

Prayer: *Father today I will be transformed by the renewing of my mind that I may prove what is your good acceptable and perfect will. I will meditate upon your word and allow the*

Holy Spirit to guide every aspect of my life.

Scriptures to Meditate: Proverbs 3:5-6, Romans 12:2

Notes

Notes

Notes

Day 22

ADORATION

Let today be a day that you limit your requests of God and just maintain an attitude of adoration!

Webster's Dictionary defines the word adoration as "the act of adoring." The word adore is defined as "**1:** To worship or honor as a deity or as divine **2:** To regard with reverent admiration and devotion **3:** To be extremely fond of."

This is the attitude David expressed in Psalm 8 when he said, "Oh Lord, our Lord how excellent is Your name in all the earth!"

Today meditate on the names of God. They express the very nature of God.

Elohim:	Expresses His greatness and glory
Yahweh/Jehovah:	Speaks of His eternal existence
El Shaddai:	"Almighty" expresses the powerful nature of God
Adonai:	Speaks of His ownership of His people
Jehovah Jireh:	"God will provide"
Jehovah Raphah:	"Jehovah heals"
Jehovah Nissi:	"Jehovah is my banner" my victory
Jehovah –m'Kaddesh:	"Jehovah who sanctifies"
Jehovah Shalom:	"Jehovah is peace"
Jehovah Tsidkenu:	"Jehovah our righteous"
Jehovah Rohi:	"The Lord is my shepherd"
Jehovah Shammah:	"Jehovah is there"

Repeat each of these names and their meaning and make each statement personal. For example, "Jehovah Shalom, you are **my** peace, Jehovah Shammah you are always here with **me**." As you begin to receive revelation of who God is to **you**, you will experience a joy and confidence that fills your soul to which nothing can compare!

"Oh Lord, our Lord, how excellent is Your Name in all the earth!" Psalm 8:9

Write a letter to God expressing your adoration.

Notes

Day 23

WORSHIP AND BREAKTHROUGH

Breakthrough often occurs during worship. When you are in a state of worship, your focus is on Him and not on yourself or your situation. As you allow Him to increase in your life, everything else decreases. Problems don't seem so pressing, you become unselfish, your faith in Him is allowed to increase.

Worship is a **lifestyle**; it is a constant state of knowing that He is God and He loves you. A **lifestyle** of worship is a constant focus on your number one priority, HIM. Your behavior and your speech should reflect your admiration, appreciation and acknowledgement of Him.

This is worship.

When you begin to practice a **lifestyle** of worship, you will notice breakthrough in your emotions as well as divine healing and deliverance. You will gain revelation in areas in which you are seeking answers.

Repeat aloud: ***Nothing and no one is more important to me than You Lord. My relationship with You is my most valuable possession!***

Repeat this confession throughout the day

Scripture to meditate: Psalm 32:7

Notes

Day 24

FEED YOUR SPIRIT

"Finally, my brethren, be strong in the Lord and in the power of His might" (Ephesians 6:10).

Some of us spend more time feeding our flesh than feeding our spirit. **Whatever you feed the most becomes the strongest.** This is why our flesh may at times override our spirit. If we give in to every whim or desire of the flesh, carnality will prevail in our lives instead of spirituality. To be carnal is to be spiritually immature. We must learn to deny our flesh so that we don't become subject to our flesh.

The more you deny your body certain foods, the

more weight you lose. You must learn to deny the carnal mind of its desires, such as being lazy or complacent, complaining about circumstances and criticizing others, so that you may lose the "weight" of carnality. When you deny your flesh, its desires begin to decrease.

Begin to exercise spiritually so that you may be strengthened with might through Christ Jesus!
- Give thanks
- Pray always
- Rejoice always
- Study the word
- Pray in the spirit
- Fast
- Attend church services

Questions to ponder:
1. *Am I doing my "spiritual exercises" regularly?* (see above)
2. *Are there any areas of my life in which carnality prevails?*

Scriptures to Meditate: Romans 8:5-8, 1 Corinthians 3:1-3, Ephesians 6:10

Answer the following questions:

Am I doing my spiritual exercises? Are there any areas of my life in which carnality prevails?

Notes

Day 25

GOD WANTS YOU!

As the statement goes, "Uncle Sam wants you," I would say to you today, **GOD** wants you! He wants <u>all</u> of you though; He wants total commitment. You need to have the same willingness that the disciples had when He called them. They left everything and everyone to follow Him. He must maintain first place in your life. Your relationship with Him must be your most important relationship. You must endeavor to do His will, not your own. You must surrender every aspect of your mind, will and emotions, so that you can follow Him.

What are you holding on to, and what are you

unwilling to give up? What is keeping you from totally surrendering with all your heart to Him? Don't be a slave to your mind, will and emotions; but become a bondslave (a willing slave) of Jesus Christ. **Go ahead lose yourself in Him!**

Scriptures to Meditate: Matthew 10:37-39

Answer the following question:

Is there anything that is keeping you from totally surrendering all of your heart to Him?

Notes

Notes

Notes

Day 26

DON'T LOSE FAITH

A Prophetic Word

"Why have you given up, why are you losing heart? Don't you remember what I have promised? Just because it has not happened yet does not mean that I have said no, or that I have forgotten! My promises are yes and if I said it, it is so. You must pass every test before going to the next level. It is because of my love for you that I am protecting you from yourself! You must be tested and proven so that you will be successful. Take the test, accept the trial; I am with you every step of the way! You shall spring forth as a new creature; enjoy the process!"

Scripture to Meditate: Philippians 1:6 *"Being confident of this very thing, that He who has begun a good work in you will complete it until the day of Jesus Christ"*

Notes

Notes

Day 27

KNOW THE TRUTH

Strongholds are mindsets that are developed as a result of a lie that the devil has convinced one to believe. God's Word says "whatsoever is true… think on these things" (Philippians 4:8). Believing the lies of the enemy will cause you to remain in a personal prison. Are you afraid of failure or success? Do you struggle to see yourself as God sees you? Do you have trouble trusting others? Are you holding on to past hurts? Do you lack confidence?

If you have remained a prisoner of any false mindset, today is the day to ask God to renew your mind by His word. His Word is the truth! He is the Truth, the whole

Truth, and nothing but the Truth! Begin to confess today that you have the mind of Christ. Pray that the Lord will allow you to see people and situations as He sees them!

List any strongholds that are imprisoning your mind

_____

_____

_____

_____

Prayer: *"Today, Lord open my eyes to the truth!"*
Scripture to Meditate: Philippians 4:8

Answer the following questions:

Have I abandoned the simple life? If so, in what way? Am I living above my means? Am I getting the proper rest?

Notes

Day 28

FORGET ABOUT YOURSELF!

I am reminded of the words to a popular worship song, "Forget about yourself, concentrate on Him and worship Him." Those words must become a lifestyle for those who are a part of the kingdom of God. You must remember that it is not about you, but it is about Him. You are not the focus of your world; but He who created you and your world must be your focus.

He has an assignment for you and that assignment includes obeying Him, keeping His commandments, loving Him with all your heart and loving your neighbor as yourself. None of these assignments are self-centered.

Worship is a lifestyle; worship is unselfish and God-centered. Just remember it is not about you, so *"forget about yourself, concentrate on Him and worship Him."*

Prayer: *Father, you are my source and my reason for living. My life belongs to you. I give back to you the life that you have given me. I will not be motivated by selfish ambition, but I will seek first your kingdom and its righteousness. There is no one more important to me than You. Father, I will worship You all of my days.*

Scripture to Meditate: Psalm 24

Notes

Notes

Day 29

THE SIMPLE LIFE

Four basic needs must be in operation in order to maintain quality of life. Those four needs include **1)** food **2)** shelter **3)** clothing **4)** rest. Sometimes in our efforts to have more quantity in life, we neglect the basic needs that will give us quality of life. Today we will discuss the first two needs, food and shelter.

Food

There was a time when most people grew their own food in their own yard. Families ate healthy hearty meals daily. However, our modern society, in an effort to produce more *quantity*, has decreased the quality of food by including hormones and additives. Many of these chemicals have an adverse effect on our bodies. What ever happened to the simple life?

Shelter

There was a time when individuals built their own homes or saved money for years and paid cash to purchase a home. Then something called credit came along and allowed people to purchase homes that they could not truly afford. They would then spend the rest of their lives indebted to the creditor. A vicious cycle was then created allowing people to buy bigger homes, accumulate more debt and in turn work more hours, spending less time with family. What happened to the simple life?

Society's efforts to make life "easier" have eliminated **simple** God-given wisdom. God has promised to provide all of our needs; however, greed and selfishness have caused us to hinder that which He has provided.

Questions to Consider:

In what ways have I allowed my desire for quantity to decrease my quality of life? _____

_____

_____

_____

_____

Have I allowed a fast-paced lifestyle to hinder me from caring for my body, which is the temple of the Holy Spirit?

_____

_____

_____

In what ways, if any, am I living above my means?

_____

_____

_____

Notes

Notes

Day 30

THE SIMPLE LIFE

Today we will discuss the last two basic needs, clothing and rest.

Clothing

There was a time when women would make clothes for themselves and their family. Everyone had the proper clothing for each season. Whoever thought there would come a time when a dress would cost as much as a car! Whoever thought there would come a time when people would define themselves by the clothes that they wear and allow themselves to purchase certain name brands that are unaffordable to them. Where did we go wrong?

Rest

There was a time when businesses would close on Sunday so that everyone could honor the Lord of the Sabbath and take time to rest. In certain cultures, there are specific hours during the day when rest is ordered. There was a time when families went to bed when the sun went down. Whoever thought there would be so many sleep-deprived individuals. Why do we compare resting to laziness? Since when did it become unusual for individuals to take time to rest?

Luke 8:14 speaks of how the "cares, riches, and pleasures of life," choke the word that is sown into the "ground" of our heart. One of the greatest traps that the enemy sets is that of hurriedness/busyness. People no longer practice delayed gratification. Everything must happen in an instant. The fast- paced lifestyle has created nothing but stress, disease, poor nutrition, lack of prioritizing, lack of care and concern for others, lack of time for the things that matter most in life and the list goes on!

I realize that we live in a modern society with new technology. I am not suggesting that we return to a primitive lifestyle, I am merely acknowledging the fact that some of the modern conveniences have caused us to abandon some of the vital basics of quality of life. In our efforts to have more and do more, we sometimes neglect the most precious people and things in our life; namely God and family.

Take a moment and examine your life. Have you abandoned the simple things that cause quality of life; or have you allowed your desire for quantity to choke the life out of those things that matter most and choke the Word that God has sown in your heart. I challenge you to get back to the basics. Maintain healthy eating habits, do not live above your means, and allow time for rest and relaxation! Allow your life to be "good ground," bearing much fruit!

Scriptures to Meditate: Luke 8:11-15

Notes

Notes

Day 31

COME TO ME

A Prophetic Word

"Trust Me, Seek Me, Worship Me, Commune with Me!"

"Beloved, It is my desire that you would trust Me. Just as you know that your chair will hold you when you sit down, you have extreme confidence as you sit, sometimes you don't even look first, you just sit knowing that your chair will hold you and that it will not break or be pulled out from underneath you. How much more should you trust

Me, your creator, lover of your soul. I desire that you trust Me without thinking twice. Let trusting Me become as natural as breathing.

Seek Me with all your heart and you will find the thing that you long for. Whatever you need, I am already aware and have made provision, but you must come to Me, you must seek Me. Look for Me as you would look for a hidden treasure.

Worship Me let Me know of My worth to you. Commune with Me, My friend. I desire fellowship, your time, your focus, I desire you!"

Scripture to Meditate: Psalm 34:1-4, 8

Notes

Notes

ABOUT THE AUTHOR

Renita Collins is a wife, mother, homemaker, business owner, singer and songwriter. She is also a partner in ministry with her husband Frank Collins Jr., pastor of North Star Christian Fellowship Church in St Clair Shores, Michigan. Renita has conducted many seminars for women in the areas of beauty, self-esteem and goal setting.

In addition to leading a church, Renita and her husband Frank are Human Behavior Consultants, conducting seminars that teach others how truly understand others as well as themselves in all relationships. Renita and her husband are very passionate about helping men and women achieve excellence in every area of their lives starting with their most important relationship, which is with Jesus Christ.

Renita and Frank can be reached through
North Star Christian Fellowship
P.O. Box 223
St. Clair Shores, MI 48080
(586) 771-1671
or E-mail

focus31days@yahoo.com

Praise for
31 Days of Focus

What an honor is was to have Renita ask me to read her manuscript. I have had the privilege to know her and her husband for many years; she has always been very serious about her relationship with God. As you read this book, you shall sense the anointing upon her life and love that she has for Christ Jesus.

During our times of growth and development there are many experiences that we have, some we understand; some we do not. It is during these times that we need to have an assurance that God is with us and for us. In different seasons in our life, we need comfort and assurance. This book will greatly enhance your life; each day you will receive new inspiration, new hope, understanding and peace as you enter into a time of fellowship with God.

The author stresses some very pertinent fundamental principals in developing confidence in God. As you apply these principles to your life, you will experience a life of blessedness in Jesus name. Thank God for the Holy Spirit inspiring Renita Collins to write this book.

Be blessed,

Bishop Dr. Frankie H. Young
Senior Pastor of Hope Evangelical Ministries